W9-CDE-786

Dear Parents/Caregivers:

Children learn to read in stages, and all children develop reading skills at different ages. **Fisher-Price® Ready Reader Storybooks™** were created to encourage children's interest in reading and to increase their reading skills. The stories in this series were written to specific grade levels to serve the needs of children from preschool through third grade. Of course, every child is different, so we hope that you will allow your child to explore the stories at his or her own pace.

Book 1 and Book 2: Most Appropriate For Preschoolers

Book 3 and Book 4: Most Appropriate For Kindergartners

Book 5 and Book 6: Most Appropriate For First Graders

Book 7 and Book 8: Most Appropriate For Second Graders

Book 9 and Book 10: Most Appropriate For Third Graders

All of the stories in this series are fun, easy-to-follow tales that have engaging full-color artwork. Children can move from Books 1 and 2, which have the simplest vocabulary and concepts, to each progressive level to expand their reading skills. With the **Fisher-Price® Ready Reader Storybooks™**, reading will become an exciting adventure for your child. Soon your child will not only be ready to read, but will be eager to do so.

Educational Consultants: Mary McLean-Hely, M.A. in Education: Design and Evaluation of Educational Programs, Stanford University; Wendy Gelsanliter, M.S. in Early Childhood Education, Bank Street College of Education; Nancy A. Dearborn, B.S. in Education, University of Wisconsin-Whitewater

Fisher-Price® Ready Reader Storybook™
Howard's Screechy Violin

Book 10

Written by Nancy Parent • Illustrated by Jilly Slattery

Modern Publishing
A Division of Unisystems, Inc.
New York, New York 10022

One day, Howard decided he wanted to play the violin. He went to see his music teacher at school.

"You must practice every day,"
she said.

That night, Howard took out his violin. He began to play.

His violin made lots of screechy sounds. It scared his cat, Jack. It made his dog, Sam, cry.

"Bye!" called Matt, his older brother, as he ran for the door.

"I think I left something in
the car," said Howard's dad.
His little sister, Molly, crawled
under the table.

11

The next night, the babysitter came over. When Howard played, she put her headphones over her ears.

Even Mrs. Tumble, next door,
couldn't stand the noise.

13

But Howard's mother loved to
hear him play.

She even clapped when he was done.

Every night, after dinner, Howard played his violin.

And every night, his brother, sister, dad and pets all ran away.

"Where do you think they go?"
asked Howard.
His mom just shrugged.

One night, Howard's family got tired of running away.

"Well," said Mom. "I always say… if you can't beat him, join him!"

"How?" asked Molly. "None of us can play the violin."

"What can you play?" asked Mom.

"I can play the tambourine!"
cried Molly.

"I can play the clarinet," said Matt.

"I can play the guitar," said Dad.
"I can play the piano," said Mom.

The next night, the whole family played together.

After a few weeks, they sounded really good—even Howard!

Mrs. Tumble and the babysitter joined in. Howard's family became known as Howard Clark and His Musical Larks.

Howard and his family held a concert for the neighbors. Everyone loved it!

They played at parties, picnics, and on holidays. And it all started with Howard's screechy violin.

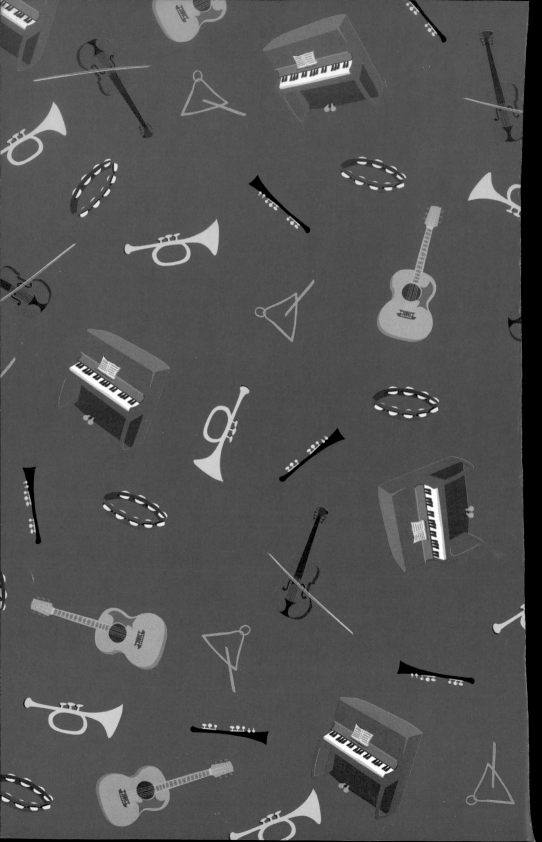